FACT PLANET

EARTH'S RESOURCES

IZZI HOWELL

W

FRANKLIN WATTS

LONDON • SYDNEY

Franklin Watts
First published in Great Britain in 2020 by the Watts Publishing Group
Copyright © the Watts Publishing Group 2020

Produced for Franklin Watts by
White-Thomson Publishing Ltd
www.wtpub.co.uk

Series Editor: Izzi Howell
Series Designer: Rocket Design (East Anglia) Ltd

HB ISBN: 978 1 4451 7279 8
PB ISBN: 978 1 4451 7280 4

All **bold** words appear in the glossary on page 30.

Franklin Watts
An imprint of
Hachette Children's Group
Part of the Watts Publishing Group
Carmelite House
50 Victoria Embankment
London EC4Y 0DZ

An Hachette UK Company
www.hachette.co.uk
www.franklinwatts.co.uk

Find the answers to all questions in this book on page 28.

Contents

What are resources? 4

Using resources 6

Oil, coal and natural gas 8

Fossil fuel problems 10

Wood 12

Trees and the environment 14

Mining 16

Water 18

Farming 20

Wildlife 22

Reducing, reusing and recycling 24

Looking after Earth's resources 26

Answers 28

Glossary 30

Further information 31

Index 32

What are resources?

There are many natural resources on Earth.

Resources come from nature. They include materials such as wood, rock and metal. We turn these **raw** materials into new materials, such as paper (from wood) and plastic (from oil), and objects, such as cars, aeroplanes and furniture.

FACT!

The raw material sand is used to make many products, including bricks, cement and even glass!

We depend on resources, such as oil and coal, for energy. We can also **generate** electricity using natural resources such as sunlight, water and wind. The food and water that we need to survive are natural resources, too.

Coal is dug out of the ground. It is used as a fuel and to generate electricity among other uses (see pages 8–9).

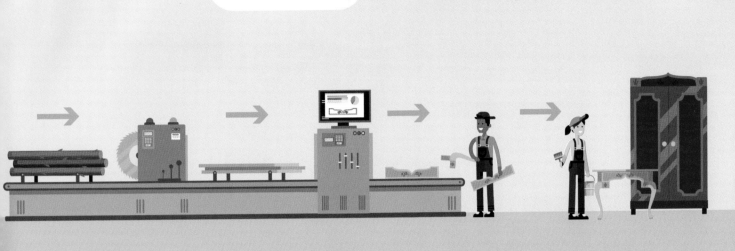

Resources can be **renewable** or **non-renewable**. Our supply of renewable resources, such as wind, will never run out. We can always grow more renewable resources, such as wood. Once we use up the non-renewable resources on Earth, such as coal, our supply will be gone. It will take millions of years for them to form again.

PICTURE PUZZLE

What is this non-renewable resource?

Using resources

In some countries, people use more resources than in others.

People in more economically developed countries (MEDCs) tend to use more resources than people in less economically developed countries (LEDCs). They usually live in larger houses that contain more objects, require more resources to build and more energy to heat and cool.

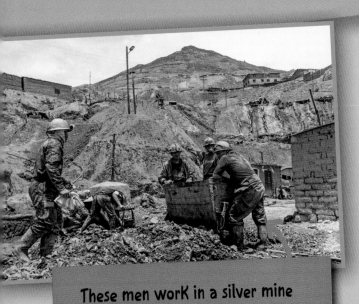

These men work in a silver mine in Bolivia, South America.

Many raw materials come from LEDCs. People in these countries work gathering these resources, often in dangerous conditions. The raw materials are often sold to MEDCs for a low price.

PICTURE PUZZLE

The raw ingredients for this food are grown in LEDCs. What food is it?

The use of resources is connected to population. The more people on Earth, the more resources we need to support the population. We think that the world population is going to get much larger in the future. There may not be enough resources to go around, especially as some people are already using many more resources than others.

FACT!

People in MEDCs use up to **10 times** more resources than those living in LEDCs.

Oil, coal and natural gas

Oil, coal and natural **gas** are used as fuels and to generate electricity. Oil is also used to make plastic.

Coal, oil and natural gas are known as fossil fuels. They formed underground over millions of years from the remains of dead animals or plants.

Oil forms from the remains of dead sea animals.

FACT!

Around **80 per cent** of the world's energy comes from fossil fuels.

QUESTION TIME

WHICH FOSSIL FUEL IS A LIQUID?

a Natural gas

b Oil

c Coal

We dig mines to access coal. Machines or mine workers dig it out of the ground. We access oil and natural gas by digging deep holes in the ground and using pumps to draw them up to the surface.

Oil and natural gas are often found under the sea bed. Boats collect the resources from the pumps in oil rigs and take them to shore.

Fossil fuels are burned in power plants to power a machine that generates electricity. Electricity from power plants is sent to homes and businesses. Burning fossil fuels is bad for the environment (see pages 10–11).

Fossil fuel problems

Using fossil fuels to generate electricity leads to many problems.

When fossil fuels are burned, they release a gas called **carbon dioxide**. This gas gathers in the **atmosphere** around Earth and traps heat from the Sun close to the surface. This makes the temperature on Earth increase. This is known as the greenhouse effect. The greenhouse effect leads to **extreme** weather and makes it hard for plants and animals to survive.

greenhouse gases in the atmosphere

Burning fossil fuels also creates air pollution. Breathing in air pollution is bad for people's health. It can cause lung problems and diseases such as cancer.

Fossil fuels are non-renewable resources. Once we use up all the fossil fuels on Earth, there won't be any more for millions of years. We will have to find other ways to power vehicles and generate electricity, such as using wind power or solar power. It's also important to stop using fossil fuels before we run out to protect the environment.

Wind turbines are used to generate electricity. They are better for the environment as they don't release carbon dioxide or pollution. We will also never run out of wind.

FACT!

If we carry on using the same amount of oil **(11 billion tonnes** a year), we may run out by 2052.

Wood

Trees are cut down for wood.

Cutting down trees is called logging. After trees are cut down, they are sent to sawmills, where they are cut into different size pieces, depending on what they are going to be used for.

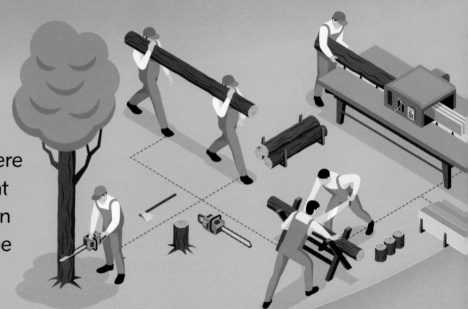

Wood is used for many things. It is used as a material in buildings and furniture. It is also **processed** and made into paper. In LEDCs, wood is used as a fuel for heating and cooking.

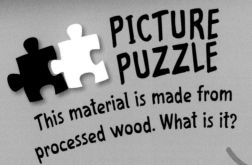

PICTURE PUZZLE

This material is made from processed wood. What is it?

Over
80,000
sheets of paper
can be made from
one average
pine tree!

A lot of the wood that we use comes from trees that have been planted to use as this kind of resource. This is a **sustainable** way of using wood, as we can plant and grow more trees to replace the ones that we use. However, cutting down wild forests for wood creates many problems (see pages 14–15).

This wood comes from a pine **plantation**.

Trees and the environment

Removing certain trees can create environmental problems.

Cutting down trees for wood in wild forests, such as rainforests, is very bad for the environment. It destroys the **habitats** of the animals and plants that live there. People and animals who depend on forest plants for food go hungry.

QUESTION TIME

WHICH OF THESE ANIMALS LIVES IN THE RAINFOREST?

a Orangutan

b Lion

c Polar bear

Trees are also very important to the environment because they clean the air by absorbing carbon dioxide and releasing **oxygen**. Cutting down trees means that less carbon dioxide is absorbed from the air. This makes the greenhouse effect worse (see page 10).

carbon dioxide

oxygen

For these reasons, it is illegal to cut down wild forests in most countries. However, some people still do it anyway. They sell the wood and use the cleared land for farming or to build roads.

This area of the Amazon Rainforest in South America has been cleared of its trees.

FACT!

Between 1990 and 2016, the area of forest **destroyed worldwide** could have covered the country of **South Africa.**

Mining

Rock and metal are mined from the ground.

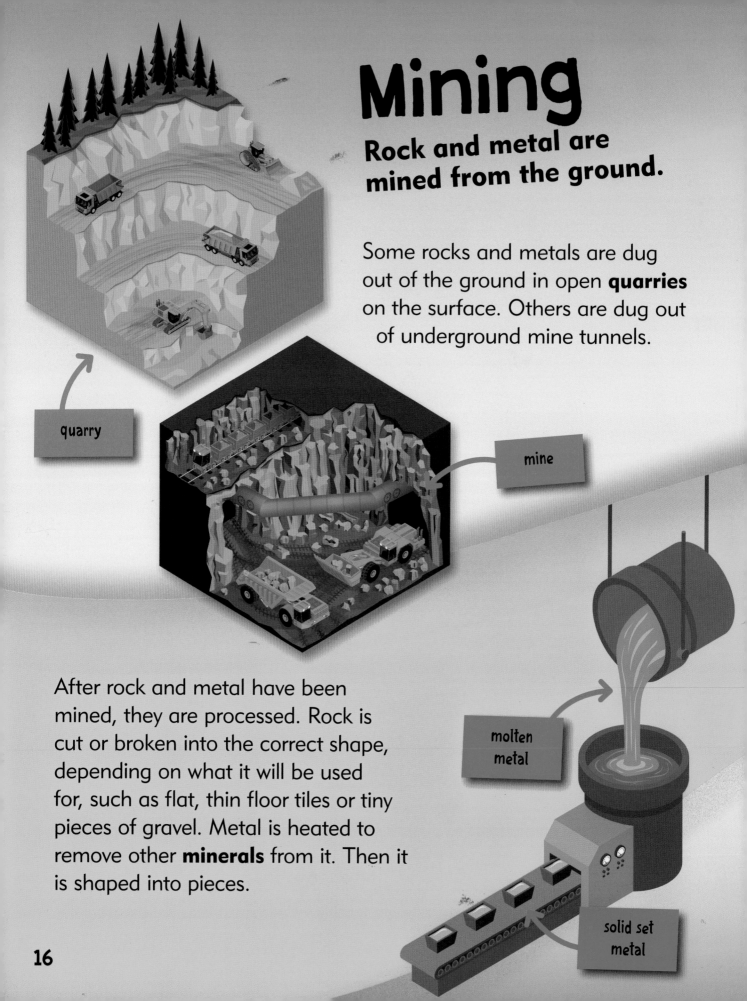

Some rocks and metals are dug out of the ground in open **quarries** on the surface. Others are dug out of underground mine tunnels.

quarry

mine

After rock and metal have been mined, they are processed. Rock is cut or broken into the correct shape, depending on what it will be used for, such as flat, thin floor tiles or tiny pieces of gravel. Metal is heated to remove other **minerals** from it. Then it is shaped into pieces.

molten metal

solid set metal

Metal doesn't just come from the ground! There are very small amounts of **gold in the ocean** but no one knows how to find and collect it.

QUESTION TIME

WHAT IS AN ORE?

a A mixture of metal and other minerals

b A very large piece of rock

c Two types of metal mixed together

Mines can damage the environment. When natural habitats are cleared to build quarries, animals lose their homes. Chemicals and waste from mining can also escape and poison the surroundings.

Pollution from a copper mine has turned this river orange.

Water
Not everyone has access to clean water.

Fresh water is a very important resource. People need it to drink, cook and clean. In many parts of the world, people have clean water piped into their homes. They use large amounts of water taking long showers and watering large gardens. A lot of this water is wasted.

FACT!

Letting the tap run for 5 minutes while washing up can waste

45 litres
of water.

PICTURE PUZZLE

Watering plants with one of these, rather than a hose, helps to save water. What is it?

These people in Ethiopia are collecting water from a lake to carry back to their homes.

In some parts of the world, people don't have enough clean fresh water. There are no water pipes and their nearby water source, such as a lake or river, has dried up or become polluted. Their only option is to walk a long way to collect water or drink dirty water.

Drinking dirty water leads to diseases. These diseases kill many people every year. To stop this from happening, water pumps that take clean water from deep underground need to be built in areas without a good source of water.

Farming

Farming helps to supply the world with food.

There aren't enough **wild** plants and animals for us to eat, so farmers grow crops and raise animals to provide food. Crops include vegetables, grains such as wheat and rice, and plants that are used for oil, such as sunflowers and olives. Animals are raised for their meat, milk and eggs.

QUESTION TIME

WHICH OF THESE FOODS IS NOT MADE FROM MILK?

a Yoghurt

b Margarine

c Butter

In some places, there is not enough food to go around. Farmers can't grow enough crops because of extreme weather, plant diseases or problems with the soil quality. Sometimes, people simply don't have the money to buy enough food.

These crops are dying because no rain has fallen in a while, and there isn't enough water for them to grow.

In other parts of the world, a lot of food goes to waste. People buy more food than they can eat and throw away leftovers. This is a huge waste of resources. To make the world fairer, MEDCs need to reduce food waste and support countries where people go hungry.

FACT!

1 in 9
people around the world don't get enough food to eat.

21

Wildlife

Wild plants and animals are important resources.

Fish are one of the most commonly eaten wild animals. They are caught from the seas, lakes and rivers. Catching too many fish, particularly young fish, is affecting fish populations. We need to leave these young fish to **reproduce** so that we will have fish in the future.

FACT!

One third of the fish species on Earth are being **overfished**.

Some wild plants contain chemicals that can be used in medicines. These plants are only found deep in rainforests and other natural habitats. It's important to protect these natural resources in case they contain the undiscovered cure for a serious disease.

Bees, butterflies and other insects **pollinate** wild plants and fields of crops. Without these insects, the plants wouldn't create fruit or new seeds. Many of these animals are at risk from **pesticides** and habitat loss. If they die out, our food supply will end.

PICTURE PUZZLE

This animal also helps to pollinate plants in some areas. What is it?

Reducing, reusing and recycling

Earth's resources are often wasted. Reusing and recycling helps us to make the most of them.

Using as few resources as possible is better for the environment. For example, reduce the amount of plastic you consume by using your own reusable bag or water bottle. Reuse the objects you already own, for example by using a jar to store leftovers rather than buying a new container.

Recycling also helps us to use fewer resources. Instead of taking new resources from nature, we take used resources and turn them into new objects. Many materials can be recycled, including paper, glass, metal and some types of plastic.

Recyclable plastic can only be recycled **2 or 3 times** before it cannot be recycled any more.

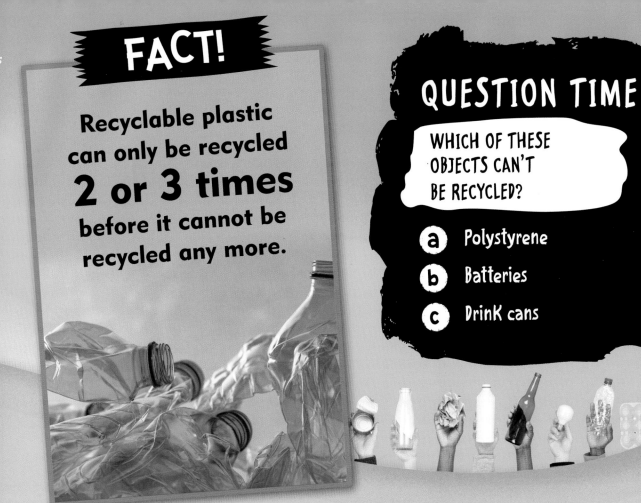

QUESTION TIME

WHICH OF THESE OBJECTS CAN'T BE RECYCLED?

a Polystyrene

b Batteries

c Drink cans

However, recycling does require energy and this can come from burning fossil fuels. This creates more environmental problems. So it's better to try to reduce the amount of resources you use before you recycle them.

Looking after Earth's resources

We need to use resources in a sustainable way to protect the environment.

Two of the biggest problems with resources are the number of people on Earth and the amount of resources that each person uses. If the world population and the amount of resources we use continue to increase, we will run out of resources and do terrible damage to the planet.

FACT!

If everyone on Earth used as many resources as the average person in the USA, we'd need the resources from

4 Earths

to support ourselves.

The most important solution is to reduce the amount of resources we use so that there are more to go around and less damage is done to the environment. Every small step helps. For example, instead of taking a long bath, why not take a quick shower?

It's important to replace and protect renewable resources, for example by replanting trees that are cut down. We also need to stop using resources that damage the environment. Wind, water and solar power can be used to generate electricity instead of fossil fuels.

solar panels

PICTURE PUZZLE

Using this vehicle instead of a car helps to save resources and the environment. What is it?

Answers

PAGE 5

Picture Puzzle:
Gold

PAGE 7

Picture Puzzle:
Chocolate

PAGE 8

Question Time!
b) Oil

PAGE 11

Question Time!
c) Asthma, a breathing disease

PAGE 12

Picture Puzzle: Cardboard

PAGE 14

Question Time! a) Orangutan

PAGE 17

Question Time!
a) A mixture of metal and other minerals

PAGE 18

Picture Puzzle:
A watering can

PAGE 20

Question Time!
b) Margarine (made from vegetable oil)

PAGE 23

Picture Puzzle:
A hummingbird

PAGE 25

Question Time!
a) Polystyrene

PAGE 27

Picture Puzzle:
A bicycle

Glossary

atmosphere the gases around Earth

carbon dioxide a gas produced when certain materials are burned or when humans and animals breathe out

extreme unusual or very intense

fuel a resource that is used to provide heat or power, usually by being burned

gas a type of substance, such as air, that is not a solid or a liquid

generate to produce

habitat the natural area where a plant or animal lives

mineral a valuable substance that is found in the ground

non-renewable describes a resource that exists in a limited quantity on Earth and will not form again for millions of years

oxygen a gas that living things need to survive

pesticide a chemical used to protect crops by killing insects and other small animals

plantation an area where trees are grown for wood

pollinate to take pollen from one plant to another so that new seeds can be produced

processed treated in a way to change a natural material into something else

quarry a hole in Earth's surface where materials are dug out of the ground

raw in a natural, unprocessed state

renewable describes a resource that can be replaced or will never run out

reproduce to have young

sustainable describes something that can be done for a long time because it doesn't damage the environment

wild describes an animal or plant that lives in nature without human interaction

Further information

Books

How Recycling Works (Eco-Works) by Geoff Barker
(Franklin Watts, 2017)

Natural Resources (Ecographics) by Izzi Howell
(Franklin Watts, 2019)

Source to Resource series by Michael Bright
(Wayland, 2018)

Websites

www.bbc.co.uk/teach/class-clips-video/primary-science-how-is-steel-made/zfnyrj6
Watch a video that shows how raw metal is turned into steel.

www.dkfindout.com/uk/science/electricity/generating-electricity/
Find out more about generating electricity and energy sources.

www.reusethisbag.com/articles/kids-guide-to-recycling/
Learn more about reusing, reducing and recycling.

Index

coal 4, 5, 8, 9

electricity 4, 8, 9, 10, 11, 27

farming 15, 20–21
fishing 22
food 4, 14, 20, 21, 22, 23
fossil fuels 8–9, 10–11, 25, 27

greenhouse effect 10, 14

less economically developed countries (LEDCs) 6, 7, 12

metal 16, 17, 24
mines 6, 9, 16, 17
more economically developed countries (MEDCs) 6, 7, 21

natural gas 8, 9
non-renewable resources 5, 11

oil 4, 8, 9, 11

paper 4, 12, 13, 24
plastic 4, 8, 24, 25
pollution 10, 11, 17
population 7, 26

quarries 16, 17

raw materials 4, 6
recycling 24, 25
renewable resources 5, 13, 27
rock 4, 16, 17

solar power 4, 11, 27

water 4, 18–19, 21, 27
wildlife 10, 14, 17, 22–23
wind 4, 5, 11, 27
wood 4, 5, 12–13, 14, 15

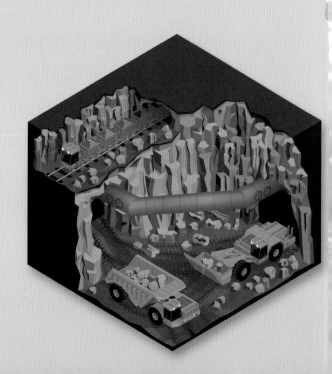

More titles in the the **Fact Planet** series

Animals at risk
Endangered animals
Biodiversity
Pollution
Habitat loss
Climate change
Hunting
Food chains
Consequences
Extinction
Saving animals
Success stories
Answers

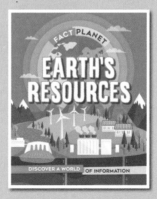

What are resources?
Using resources
Oil, coal and natural gas
Fossil fuel problems
Wood
Trees and the environment
Mining
Water
Farming
Wildlife
Reducing, reusing and recycling
Looking after Earth's resources
Answers

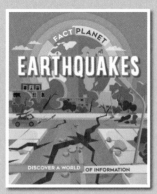

What is an earthquake?
Under the ground
Between plates
Shock waves
Measuring earthquakes
Dangers
Protecting buildings
Living with earthquakes
Tsunamis
Landslides
Predicting earthquakes
Major earthquakes
Answers

What is a mountain?
Formation
Fold mountains
Block mountains
Around the world
Erosion
Avalanches
Volcanoes
Climate
Wildlife
People and mountains
Record-breakers
Answers

What is pollution?
Air pollution
The greenhouse effect
Climate change
Acid rain
Water pollution
Ocean rubbish
Noise pollution
Light pollution
Rubbish
Reduce, reuse, recycle
Cleaning up
Answers

Rivers and coasts
The water cycle
The source
River erosion
Meanders
The mouth
Major rivers
Coast habitats
Tides
Coasts and erosion
Floods
People and water
Answers

What is a settlement?
Types of settlement
Settlement sites
Settlement patterns
Parts of a settlement
Settlement density
Facilities
Homes
Problems in settlements
Changing settlements
Megacities
Extreme settlements
Answers

What is a volcano?
Formation
Location
Eruption
Shapes of volcano
Lava
Volcanic rock
Underwater volcanoes
Predicting eruptions
Volcanoes and people
Geothermal energy
Major volcano eruptions
Answers